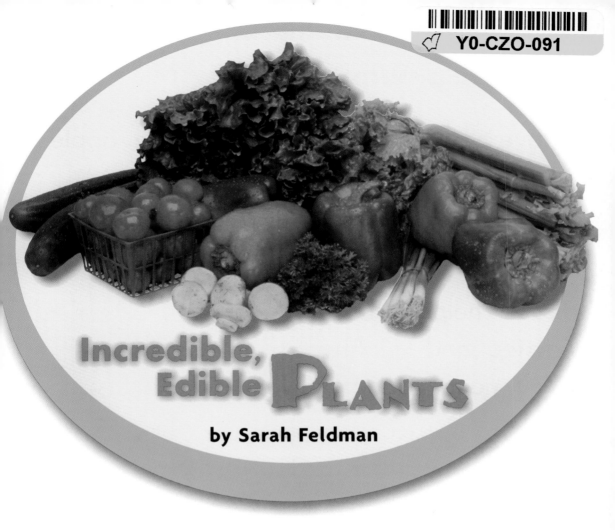

Incredible, Edible PLANTS

by Sarah Feldman

Table of Contents

Are You What You Eat?

Have you heard the saying, "An apple a day keeps the doctor away"? Have you heard that "you are what you eat"?

Food helps your body stay active and healthy. You need food to live.

Food is fuel for your body. The healthier your food, the better you feel!

To stay healthy, your body needs **nutrients**. Nutrients are found in food. Nutrients give you the energy you need to run, move around, and even think and read. They give your body everything it needs to work and grow.

Different nutrients are found in different foods. You can get all the nutrients you need by eating a well-balanced **diet**. A well-balanced diet includes many different foods, such as fruit, vegetables, bread, meat, beans, and milk.

Eating a well-balanced diet every day helps you feel great.

The **food pyramid** helps you eat a well-balanced diet. It has five main food groups. The pyramid shows how many **servings** you need to eat from each group to stay healthy.

The groups you need to eat foods from most often are fruits, vegetables, and bread and cereal. Did you know that the foods in these groups come from plants?

To learn more about these food groups, you'll need to learn about plants.

fruit   vegetable   bread

6

Food Pyramid

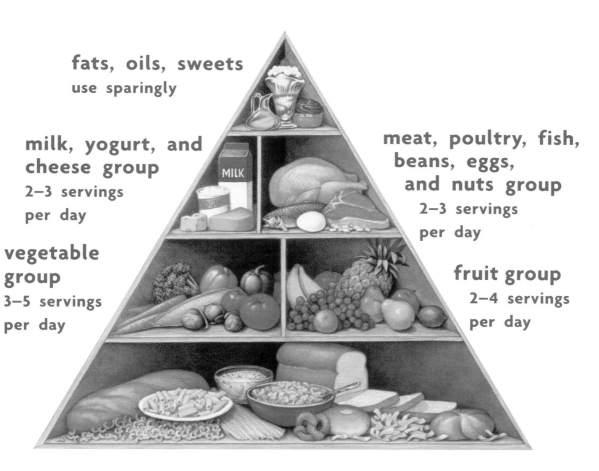

fats, oils, sweets
use sparingly

milk, yogurt, and
cheese group
2–3 servings
per day

meat, poultry, fish,
beans, eggs,
and nuts group
2–3 servings
per day

vegetable
group
3–5 servings
per day

fruit group
2–4 servings
per day

MILK

bread, cereal, rice, and pasta group
6–11 servings per day

What Parts of Plants Do You Eat?

Most plants have roots, stems, leaves, and seeds. Many plants also have flowers and fruits. When you eat fruits, vegetables, and **grains**, you eat one of these plant parts.

Each plant part helps keep the plant alive. Each part has nutrients that your body uses to stay healthy.

leaves

flowers

fruit

stem

seeds

roots

9

What foods come from plants?
Let's find out.

Foods That Come From Plant Parts

Roots	beet, carrot, radish, turnip, potato
Stems	asparagus, celery
Leaves	cabbage, lettuce, kale, spinach
Seeds	bread, cereal, corn, crackers, flour, nuts, pasta, peas, rye, wheat
Fruits	apple, berries, lemon, cucumber, orange, mango, melon, pear, pepper, pumpkin, squash, tomato
Flowers	broccoli, cauliflower

Vegetables such as carrots, potatoes, beets, and turnips are the roots of plants.

The roots of a plant keep the plant in the ground. The roots take in nutrients and water from the soil that the plant needs.

beets

radishes

turnip

potatoes

11

When you eat vegetables such as asparagus and celery, you are eating the stems of plants.

The stem of a plant takes the water and nutrients to different parts of the plant. It also holds up the leaves and flowers of the plant.

asparagus

celery

When you eat vegetables such as lettuce, spinach, and cabbage, you are eating the leaves of plants.

The leaves of a plant make energy so the plant can grow.

spinach

lettuce

cabbage

Foods such as nuts, corn, and peas are the seeds of plants. The seeds of a plant grow and turn into new plants.

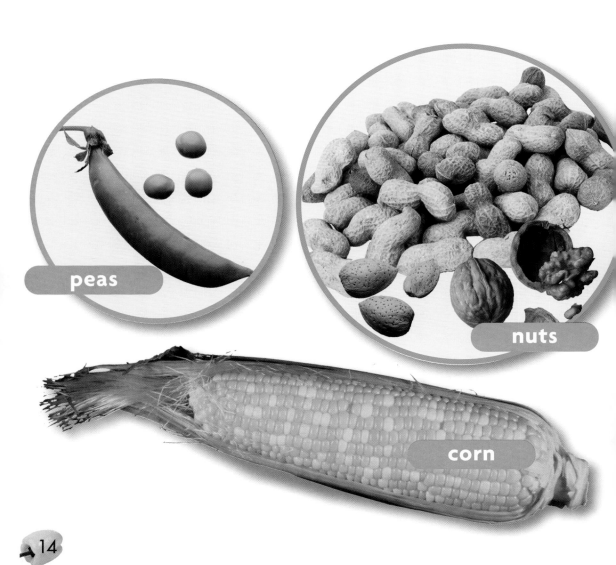

peas

nuts

corn

Bread, cereal, crackers, and pasta are made from the seeds of plants. These foods are made with flour. Flour is made by grinding seeds from plants such as wheat and rye into powder.

bread

wheat

flour

pasta

When you eat foods like apples, oranges, tomatoes, and cucumbers, you are eating the fruits of plants.

All fruits have seeds inside. Fruits have a lot of sugar and energy that seeds need in order to grow.

tomato

Some foods that we call vegetables are actually the fruits of a plant. That means that they hold the plant's seeds.

cucumber

pumpkin

squash

apple

When you eat foods such as cauliflower and broccoli, you are eating the flowers of plants.

Flowers make plant seeds. When seeds start to form, flowers turn into fruits that help the seeds grow.

cauliflower

broccoli

Plants are an important part of a healthy and well-balanced diet.

Here are two tasty snacks that can help you keep a well-balanced diet.
Can you name the plant parts used to make them?

Jammy Treats

INGREDIENTS

8 crackers

strawberry jam

1. Place four crackers on a plate.
2. Spread a small spoonful of jam on each cracker.
3. Place a second cracker on top of each cracker.
4. Enjoy!

Stuffed Celery

INGREDIENTS

celery

peanut butter

1. Wash two celery stalks.
2. Carefully spread some peanut butter on the stalks with the back of a spoon.
3. Enjoy!

Glossary

diet (DYE-ut): the foods you eat

food pyramid (FOOD PEER-a-mid): a diagram that shows the food groups and how much of each group you should eat

grain (GRAYN): the seed of a plant, such as wheat and rye, that is used to make bread and cereal

nutrients (NOO-tree-ents): things in foods, such as vitamins and minerals, that the body needs to work and grow

serving (SIR-ving): an amount of food

Index